First published in 2009 by
Zest Books, an imprint of Orange Avenue Publishing
35 Stillman Street, Suite 121, San Francisco, CA 94107
www.zestbooks.net

Created and produced by Zest Books, San Francisco, CA
© 2009 by Zest Books and Orange Avenue Publishing LLC

Typeset in Rotis, American Typewriter, and Amplifier

Teen Nonfiction / Social Issues / Adolescence

Library of Congress Control Number: 2008934372
ISBN-13: 978-0-9790173-5-3
ISBN-10: 0-9790173-5-1

CREDITS
EDITORIAL DIRECTOR: Karen Macklin
CREATIVE DIRECTOR: Hallie Warshaw
ART DIRECTOR: Tanya Napier
WRITERS: Erin Elisabeth Conley, Karen Macklin, Jake Miller
ADDITIONAL RESEARCH: Nikki Roddy
COVER DESIGN: Tanya Napier
DESIGN AND PRODUCTION: Cari McLaughlin
TEEN ADVISORY BOARD: Atticus Graven, Lisa Macklin, Andrea Mufarreh,
                    Trevor Nibbi, Sasha Schmitz

Printed in Canada
First printing, 2009
10 9 8 7 6 5 4 3 2 1

# crap

## How to deal with annoying teachers, bosses, backstabbers, and other stuff that stinks

Erin Elisabeth Conley
Karen Macklin
Jake Miller

# Table of Contents

We've all got some crap in our lives. Maybe your dad gives you crap for the clothes you wear. Maybe your mom gives it to you because you keep your room the way you like it (messy). Or, perhaps it's your math teacher, who, for whatever reason, doesn't like when you do your homework in bright purple ink (would he prefer you not do it at all?). Some days, crap just seems to be everywhere. It can come at you from all directions ... or from out of nowhere. It might come in one big dump or in little dumplings. And just when you think you have it under control, it'll appear in some new, totally unexpected form.

Crap is annoying, but it doesn't have to ruin your day — or your life, for that matter. The trick is identifying what type of crap it is and then knowing whether to avoid it, deal with it, or simply get rid of it. To start getting a handle on your crap, just sniff (uh, read) on.

**crap** *(krap)* vulgar slang (n)

**1.** excrement; an act of defecating.

**2.** foolish, deceitful, or boastful language; cheap or shoddy material; miscellaneous or disorganized items; clutter; insolent talk or behavior.

**3.** anything you would simply rather not deal with.

# What Is
# This Crap?

1

Before you can understand what to do with crap, you need to know how to identify it. This is where the science of crapology comes in. Becoming a skilled crapologist — that is, learning how to distinguish one type of crap from another — can help you anticipate what may be coming your way. That can make the crap easier to contend with, or avoid entirely. Here are the four basic types of crap.

## 1. Crap From the Management

This type comes from parents, teachers, bosses, and anyone who has authority over you. Common complaints are directed at marathon IM and video game-playing sessions, homework handed in late, tardiness to work, and other random "problems." For instance, you might get crap for hardly ever being home one week, and for hardly ever leaving your room the next.

Management crap can turn particularly nasty if comparisons become a part of it – which is all about being judged, usually against someone else or someone else's idea of who you are (or aren't). You might be compared to your sibling, the class brainiac, the school suck-up, your tennis team partner, or the community do-gooder. You may get slammed for how much better "young people used to be back in the day" – or even for not living up to your own former behavior. This twist on crap sucks for a whole slew of reasons, especially because it basically discounts all of the great qualities you actually *do* have.

## 2. Crap From Your Peers

This is the crap that comes from people about the same age as you. Think of all those backstabbing friends, jealous or cheating significant others, lame coworkers who won't cover for you when you need a day off, and siblings who steal your stuff or rat you out to your parents whenever they catch you doing something you're not supposed to be doing.

### 3. Crap From Yourself

This is one of the most common forms of crap, and it's the one you are probably most blind to (people generally think that crap is thrust upon them by external forces). This type appears in many forms, the harshest of which is self-criticism (see page 50). You are a fan of this kind of crap if you berate yourself for: failing a test even when you studied for it, disappointing a friend or parent, locking yourself out of the house or car, losing your brother's favorite watch, or being a few pounds overweight or underweight. You can also give yourself crap by behaving in a way that you know will adversely affect your life (i.e., acting like a jerk, stealing your best friend's boyfriend/girlfriend, or partying the night before a history final).

## 4. Crap From the Universe

Some people refer to this as "bad luck" (or even bad karma — see page 84). Examples: Your prom is scheduled for the same weekend as your family's (obligatory) annual reunion; your bunny dies from some rare disease that affects .0001 percent of all bunnies; you come down with the flu the night before your date with the guy/girl you have been eyeing for two years.

## What Exactly Is Crap?

**75%**
water

**30%**
dead bacteria

**30%**
indigestible food matter

**10-20%**
cholesterol and other fats

**10-20%**
inorganic substances

**2-3%**
protein

# Why People Give Crap

ou can't always stop people from dumping on you, but you can try to understand why they do it, which might rein in their stink a bit. In fact, when you stop (or stoop) to examine the situation, you may find that the people dishing you crap may even have a somewhat constructive motive. They often mean to help—no matter how misguided or lame their delivery may be. And sometimes they dish it out because they themselves are receiving or have received lots of it in the past. Here are a few reasons why people give you crap.

- They like you (maybe even *really* like you).

- They don't like you.

- They don't like themselves.

- They're projecting their own fears, ideas, hopes, dreams, or insecurities on to you.

- Their favorite  contestant was cut from *Americal Idol.*

- They want you to succeed.

- They are overworked, underpaid, sleep-deprived, and/or just generally frazzled.

- Picking on you is easier than dealing with their own crap.

- Starbucks was closed.

## Etymology of Crap

Legend has it that the word *crap* was derived from the name of Thomas Crapper, a plumber from late 19th-century England who is rumored to have created the first flush toilet. But many scholars now say that someone else invented the first modern potty. Another theory is that the word crap came from Middle English in the 1400s, when it meant "weeds" or "bad grain" (i.e., "there's a lot of crap in the field").

In the end, no one is totally sure how the common usage of crap came to be, but most agree that the concept crosses all language and cultural boundaries.

## The Crap Plants Give Us

Plants excrete oxygen as a waste product during photosynthesis, the process they use to create the sugars they live on. In other words, the air that we breathe—that we need to survive—is basically a kind of crap, produced by trees and grasses on land and phytoplankton in the sea.

# That's Crap.
# Or Is It?

**D**efining crap can be tricky because a lot of what we initially think is crap may actually be good for us. The trick is telling the difference between constructive criticism and the stuff that just wastes our time and energy and gets us nowhere fast.

To figure out whether something is crap, you have to put it to the crap test. That means asking if it holds value in your life. For instance, you may feel like all those hours of practice on the free-throw line are pure crap. But if you are doing it because you want to make varsity a year early (or if you bet your dad a month of doubled allowance that you could hit 70 percent), then it's not really crap at all. In that case, it's just the unavoidable blood, sweat, and tears of working toward something. Next time something feels like crap, take a moment to really examine it. Ask yourself:

- Is there a goal behind it?

- Will it one day get you somewhere?

- Is it in some way good for you?

If you answered "yes" to any of these questions, you might not be dealing with true crap.

**66** *If you find yourself in a hole, the first thing to do is stop digging.* **99**

—Will Rogers, cowboy

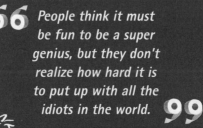

> *People think it must be fun to be a super genius, but they don't realize how hard it is to put up with all the idiots in the world.*
>
> —Calvin,
> from *Calvin and Hobbes*

# Avoiding Crap

**S**ome crap is necessary and some is even good for you, but some crap should simply be avoided. Unfortunately, it's not always possible to avoid crap, although if you adopt the right philosophy and techniques, you'll have a much better chance of not stepping in the pile set out in front of you.

## That's Nasty

Scientists believe there may be a reason why humans are disgusted by the look and smell of excrement: to keep us away from the toxins and infectious diseases that can sometimes be present in waste. This just goes to show that steering clear of crap is beneficial to our general health.

# Choose Your Battles Wisely

ou're pissed and want to do something about it. But before you act, think about how much crap will come from the fight you are about to start. It might seem pointless, cowardly, or weak to not let the other person know just how monumentally *off* they are. But your time is precious; do you really want to waste it arguing with someone who doesn't know what he or she is talking about (or is just too stubborn to see it any other way)? Sometimes the bravest and smartest thing you can do is bite your tongue and let the issue pass.

This doesn't mean you should sacrifice your values – it's important to stick up for what's truly important to you. But many of the things we find ourselves arguing about are not actually that important to us. And in those cases, simply let those difficult people win, because the sooner they believe they've won, the sooner you can go back to life as scheduled.

## Poop Happens

In May 2008, a New York woman filed a $100 claim against the city of Norwalk, Connecticut, for crap reparations. She stated that, during a family outing to Norwalk's Maritime Aquarium, her 1-year-old son stepped in dog poop, ruining the family outing — and her son's shoes. (The little boy obviously knew nothing about avoiding crap.)

Those at the city offices said they thought the claim was silly. City attorney M. Jeffry Spahr said: "The official response is: Her claim is denied and poop happens."

## A Mother Load of Crap

If you really want to avoid crap, don't go to the jungles of Asia. An Asian elephant dumps approximately 500 pounds of it per day. Think of your own body weight and figure out how many of you just one of those elephants can unload.

# Stay Away From Crap-Happy People

A goose poops every seven minutes. Some people are like geese: They're so full of crap that it seems like there's something spewing out of them every time you turn around. It could be a "friend" who always complains about the rest of the people in your group, a relative who regularly makes you feel like dirt, or a teacher who gets off on making students feel stupid. The more time you spend with crap-happy people, the more likely you are to step in something nasty. Instead, try to surround yourself with people who bring positive energy to a room, make other people feel comfortable, and choose to steer clear of useless crap as much as you can.

Sometimes, it's easy to put this into action. For instance, the next time you are at a party and everyone is talking trash about a kid who's not there — a kid who's maybe even a friend of yours — point out that person's good attributes, or say that you feel uncomfortable talking trash about someone who's not there. If your comments are met with laughter, exit stage left and find someone else to talk to.

Escaping the negativity of crap-friendly adults is a little harder, especially if they are people you have to deal with every day. In those situations, it's best to just do what you need to do for them as efficiently as you can, so you can move on to something else.

# Avoid
# Unrequired Crap

**W**ay (way) back in the day, an Italian economist named Vilfredo Pareto discovered something called the 80:20 paradigm: He realized that 20 percentof the people in the world owned about 80 percent of the wealth. This generally sucky rule works in lots of other ways, too. You'll usually find that 20 percent of the work you do earns you 80 percent of your money, or that the most annoying 20 percent of the people you know cause 80 percent of your grief.

How does this apply to you? One way to reduce the amount of crap in your life is to learn to pinpoint which crap matters most in a given situation and to focus on that instead of *all* of the crap in the universe. To apply this philosophy, pay careful attention to the feedback you get from people around you. If all your dad cares about is your room staying clean, don't spend whole weekends mowing the lawn. If your classroom participation counts for 80 percent of your grade, make sure you ask and answer lots of questions in class. If you know that one teacher drives you nuts, rearrange your schedule to avoid her class next year. It's not weaseling or copping out – it's efficiency at its finest.

> **"** *Weaseling out of things is important to learn. It's what separates us from the animals ... except the weasel.* **"**
>
> —Homer Simpson, from *The Simpsons*

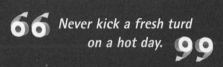

> **66** *Never kick a fresh turd on a hot day.* **99**
>
> —Harry S. Truman,
> former US president

# Don't Stir Up Crap for Yourself

hen we stop to think about it, most of us realize that we create a lot of our own crap. If your coach screamed at you for being late to a scrimmage *again*, or your mom snatched your car keys for a week after you got yet another parking ticket, then you might be tempted to blame that crap on *them* (see page 86). But deep down you know that your bad habits, like being late (to everything) and parking at meters (when you have no quarters), are what screw you in the first place.

The people around you are dealing you enough crap, so the less crap you generate for yourself, the better. The smart thing to do? Break those crap-inducing habits. Set your alarm 10 minutes earlier or remember to keep some spare quarters in your car's ashtray. These kinds of small intentional changes are surprisingly hard to make (you may already know this from personal experience), but you have to be diligent. Over time, you'll find that things in life flow more smoothly when you're not always sabotaging yourself.

# Dealing
# With Crap

As much as you may wish it would just go away, some crap is simply unavoidable. You have to deal with that annoying teacher because she is the one grading you all semester. And there's no way you could have prevented breaking your leg right before this season's tryouts.

This kind of crap — the kind you can't sidestep or ignore — demands attetion. In these unfortunate cases, there's just one thing to do: Suck it up and deal.

## Crap in Outer Space

Astronauts wear high-tech diapers to allow themselves to work uninterrupted in space for hours at a time. This is a good reminder that, in order to get stuff done, sometimes you need to put up with a whole lot of crap.

# Count on Others

ou have crap and you need help, and asking friends to break out their shovels for you is a beautiful thing. If you're a good friend, the type that frequently lends a hand to others in need, you probably won't have any problems finding help in return. Don't be proud: Get people to help you with your crap. To make crap-dealing a community effort, try these tactics.

### 1. **Do a crap swap.**

Promise to do something generous in return
for your friend's support — offer to give her
a lift to school every day or study with
her in a subject you are acing.

### 2. **Have a get-crap-done party.**

Whether you need to clean out the garage
or supervise your little sister's playgroup,
crap is more fun with company (and help).
Order a bunch of pizzas, turn up the music,
and ask your buddies to head over.

### 3. **Ask nicely (or beg).**

When you really need a hand with
something, it's best to be straightforward
and honest. You'll find that your true
friends will be happy to get involved.

# Visualize Your Way Away From Crap

At those times when crap is unavoidable, the human brain comes in very handy. You can get through tough moments by envisioning the person giving you crap in a funny or compromising situation. Actors do this all the time to quell stage fright. They imagine their audience is naked. The difference is that you're not trying to overcome any kind of fear; you're finding a way to tolerate an intolerable situation by summoning a bit of private humor.

So, for instance, say your new boss wants you to know that she is watching how much ice cream you put in every cone. You can't quit—you need this summer job to pay for your car insurance. Instead, picture a little drizzle of something nasty falling on her head every time she stares at you. Or when your history teacher is screaming, imagine that he is a duck and all you can hear is him quacking.

Remember: Half the skill in this type of visualization comes from keeping what you're doing on the down low. The expression on your face should never reflect what is going on in your mind. You should look sufficiently serious, and not like a maniacal joker or a person with anger issues.

# Take It Easy on Yourself

**S**ome of the worst kind of crap is self-criticism. Maybe you beat yourself up about that extra 5 pounds you (and only you) think you should lose. Or how you seem to be the one person in your AP physics class who still doesn't quite get that whole theory of relativity thing. Oh, and that cringingly dumb joke you made in front of your crush.

In reality, we tend to be our own worst critics and arch-nemeses. You may not always have control over crap that comes at you from the rest of the world, but you *can* exercise control over what you throw at yourself.

You know that nasty little voice in your head – the one that kicks you when you're down and tells you that you will never amount to anything? Tell it to shut its tiny cakehole. Say it out loud if you have to. (But make sure no one is in earshot.) Not everyone in your life is going to give you the benefit of the doubt. Be smart and, at the very least, give it to yourself.

# See the Bright Side

**S**ometimes when you're certain things couldn't possibly get worse, they do. Yep, as sad as it sounds, no matter the crap you're facing now, the next batch could always be nastier and more foul smelling. Knowing this doesn't negate your own crummy experiences and consequent feelings, but it can help you put things into perspective.

To see the brighter side of things, you first have to imagine the very worst. Like, what if those thugs had not just nicked your backpack and mountain bike, but also gotten your brand-new iPhone? Or how much worse it would have been to have been dumped for your backstabbing ex-best friend as opposed to the sexy French exchange student who'll be back eating baguettes in Paris by semester's end. And what if you had actually hit that old lady you nearly ran into during your driver's test? Or broken both legs rather than just sprained that left ankle while snowboarding?

Next time you feel overburdened by crap, remember: The good news is that the bad news could have always been worse.

# Laugh at Crap

**L**aughter is an excellent way to dismiss crap, but laughing at your crap, especially when it's bad, can be a hard thing to do alone. So, rally some friends and play King of the Krap Hill together.

This game is a great way to see who's survived the best of the worst, and to applaud them for it. The rules are simple: Everybody takes turns sharing their biggest loser moments, and whoever gets the most people to laugh wins.

If you want your game to have some structure, try framing each round with a question, such as "Who's had the worst date?" One friend might say that she thought she was on a date when the guy introduced her to his girlfriend. Another might say he was *finally* about to make his big move when his longtime crush said, "You know I like girls, right?" If you are having a particularly crappy year and think that winning at *something* will make you feel better, this game is particularly recommended.

> 66 Laughter and tears are both responses to frustration and exhaustion. I myself prefer to laugh, since there is less cleaning up to do afterward. 99
>
> — Kurt Vonnegut, American author (1922–2007)

# Make Use of Crap

**S**ometimes the best way to deal with crap is to make use of it. Animals know full well just how useful crap can be — after all, they use theirs to stake out territory. The scent of their crap tells other animals not to bring more crap into the vicinity.

The next time you are handed a load of crap, think about ways in which you can find a use for it. Is there something you can learn from it? A cool new person you can meet out of it? An opportunity for a future summer job or internship that could come out of it?

# Dealing With Crap

For instance, say you are stuck working on prom night. Simply use the time to bond with your cute new coworker. Or if you are damned to after-school detention for a week, start writing the script for your next webisode or screenplay.

Sometimes it even pays to sign up for crap. Being a coffee maid at your favorite magazine's publishing house will bring you more crap than a Montana cow ranch, but when that hard-to-get summer internship opens up, yours is the first résumé they'll read.

# Take a Stand Against Crap

**S**ometimes you know that the crap you are being dealt is not cool and that you need to rise up against it. Maybe your teacher fails you on your final paper only because the footnotes are not in the exact format she wanted. Or perhaps your boyfriend/girlfriend is insisting that you get dressed to the nines for a visit with his/her family when you hate wearing anything more sophisticated than jeans. In cases where you genuinely feel like you are in the right, take a stand. But be smart about it. Here are two tips.

1. ***Don't* lose control.** Screaming and yelling "I hate you and your crappy need for anally exact footnotes!!" or "You can take this dumb suit/icky taffeta dress and shove it!" will get you nowhere.

## 2. *Do* rationally bring your point up.

And raise it in a way that the person you
are standing up against can relate to. If
your teacher appreciates hard work, point
her toward all of the other A's you have
received and respectfully ask that she accept
the version of your final paper as is. If your
bf/gf responds to your funny side, humor-
ously explain why wearing formal shoes
will make it impossible to concentrate on
his/her dad's old high school war stories.

You won't always have success when you
take a stand – but the more you stand up for
what you believe is right, the greater chance
you have of being true to yourself and
taking less crap.

# Go Out and Fail

O ne of the biggest types of crap we end up facing is our own fear of failure: fear of failing others, failing ourselves, failing a class, losing a job, pissing off someone who's bigger and then "failing" by getting our butt kicked. We fear failure so much that we often decide to do *nothing* instead of risk failing. But if you don't take chances in life, you'll never live up to your full potential (and you'll become the recipient of more and more crap).

The best way to overcome a fear of failure is to tackle it head-on. Pick something you aren't any good at and go right out and do it in public. Sing or play guitar on the sidewalk, invent a new dance and perform it for friends, tell knock-knock jokes at an open-mic night. Observe how you actually *live* through the experience.

Then, try it with something you *want* to be good at. Fail the first time. Fail the second time. Understand that you may have to fail dozens of times before you get something right. In the days before digital, people used to say that what separated a great photographer from a good one was the size of his/her garbage can. Great photographers shoot a million images. A few of them are brilliant. The rest typically suck. Learning to fail with dignity is part of succeeding and living with less crap.

# Take Your Crap Seriously

**T**here's no doubt that crap is annoying, often epically so. But it can also be much more than that. Even the littlest, pettiest crap can eventually add up and leave you feeling overwhelmed, stressed, and even depressed.

So it's important to come up with some real coping mechanisms. Writing is a great way to get crap out of one's system, as is talking to good friends, doing something creative, listening to music, exercising, or just going for a really long walk.

If your usual de-stress methods are not working and you're still feeling really crappy — or if you find yourself toying with the idea of doing mean things to someone (your teacher, yourself, a peer, a small furry stuffed animal) — turn to a therapist, school counselor, or free teen hotline. There's no stigma around it: Lots of people see therapists. There's too much crap in our world, and we all need a little help wading through it sometimes.

# 4

## Getting Rid of Crap

You couldn't avoid it. And you are tired of dealing with it. Sometimes, you just need to get rid of it.

In a biological sense, there's not much to getting rid of crap. All organisms, from the simplest single-celled amoebas up to Homo sapiens, have some way of getting rid of the stuff that their bodies don't need anymore. Since the first sewers were built nearly 5,000 years ago in the ancient Indus valley, civilizations have been finding more and more sophisticated ways to conquer their collective crap. But you don't need a sewer pipe—or even a toilet—to get crap out of your life. Once you are good and ready, you just need to start flushing.

## Get Flushing

Some cultures take their crap disposal very seriously. In Singapore, you can be fined up to $1,000 for not flushing a public toilet.

# Eliminate Waste

One way of flushing toxic waste from your life is to reevaluate how you're spending your time. What could you eliminate right now from your life that would save you lots of trouble and not cost you anything you care about?

Think about...

- the things you're doing only to impress or appease people you don't really like and you won't remember in five years.

- the things you're doing because you've always done them — even without ever knowing why.

✳ the things you do only because you hope
they'll finally make a hard-to-please
family member happy.

● the things that clutter your physcal —
and hence mental — space (like those
purple sneakers lurking in the back of
your closet, or those already-read emails
littering your inbox).

By cutting crap out of your life, you'll
make space for things that really matter.

# Quit the Crap
# You Don't Need

nyone who ever told you that
quitters never win is a real loser —
or, at least, just plain wrong.

Sure, it's a problem if you give up every time
things get tough. But if you keep slogging
away at crap you don't like or aren't even
interested in, you're wasting valuable time
that could be better spent doing things that
really matter to you. Sometimes the only
thing to do in order to get ahead is to quit.

To quit your way to success and happiness,
ask yourself these 6 key questions.

If your answers to these questions tell
you that you're wasting your time doing
something useless, give yourself walking
papers pronto.

- What are the best things that will happen if I finish this project?

- What are the worst things that will happen if I don't finish? Think about the immediate, short-term, and long-term repercussions.

- How will I feel about myself if I don't finish?

- How will the five people I care about most feel?

- What could I be doing instead?

- How would doing this other thing make me feel about myself?

# Have a Crap Funeral

If you are older than 5, you likely have a special kind of crap that just seems to grow every year: emotional crap. But, in reality, that "crap" is a lot of ancient history. Perhaps you're still pissed that your parents never got you that motocross bike they had promised you upon announcing their divorce. Or maybe you're still mad that your best friend bought those metallic kitten heels when she *knew* you wanted them. And let's not forget how your little brother snooped around on your computer and exposed your secret obsession with *High School Musical: The Ice Tour.* The list could go on and on, right?

It's time to put all that crap where it belongs — in the past. One way to heal old wounds and rid yourself of past petty exasperations and emotional baggage is to conduct a symbolic cleansing ceremony. This can include anything from chanting and sage burning (if you're into that sort of thing) to donating some old clothes in favor of starting anew or redecorating your room with things that speak of a less crap-filled future. Then, once you feel a bit refreshed, have a ritual burial for any objects you've been hanging on to that hold bad memories, like old lousy report cards, photos of your ex, and that rejection letter from that program you were so sure you'd get in to. When you're good and "cleansed," take a deep breath and get on with your life.

## Annual Crap-Flushing Day

November 19 is World Toilet Day, a holiday established by the World Toilet Organization to bring global awareness to the lack of basic sanitation in the developing world, a problem that affects more than 2 billion people.

## Toilets on Display

If you are serious about flushing crap out of your life, you might want to visit the Sulabh International Museum of Toilets in New Delhi, India. The museum's founder also spearheaded a nonprofit sanitation organization in India and is on a mission to educate people about all of the ways one can get rid of crap.

# Write It Out of Your System

**K**eeping a journal can be one of the best ways to get crap out of your mind – and your life. It can be as simple as scribbling a few words every day on a piece of scrap paper that you keep in a folder hidden under your mattress, or as elaborate as an anonymous blog that you share with the world. You can even write furious letters to people who piss you off, and then toss them out (or burn them).

Use your journal as a toxic dumping ground and pour all of your problems into it. Just the act of writing things down helps to clear your system. Plus, when you look at it a few months from now, it will give you perspective on the crap that came before the crap you are now facing. After a while, you'll probably begin to identify a pattern in the types of crap that keep cropping up in your life — and do something about it.

> **66** *I like to write when I feel spiteful; it's like having a good sneeze.*
>
> — D. H. Lawrence,
> English author
> (1885–1930)

## Down the Shoot

Getting rid of crap is an important part of life: The average person spends three years of his or her life on the toilet.

**66** *There are two dilemmas that rattle the human skull: How do you hang on to someone who won't stay? And how do you get rid of someone who won't go?* **99**

— Danny DeVito
as Gavin,
*The War of the Roses* (1989)

# Breaking the Stank Cycle

**W**hen you're suddenly inundated with a load of crap, it's a perfectly natural reaction to try to dump it on someone else. Crap flows downhill, as they say, so every year in high school the senior bullies pick a freshman to harass because someone harassed them, or your boss treats you like dirt because his wife and kids yelled at him last night.

While it's good to understand that people often dish out crap because they are being crapped on, it's also important to *not* perpetuate the cycle by crapping on other people. In other words: Be the person who cuts crap rather than cultivates it.

## Monkey See, Monkey Doo-Doo

People are not the only ones who throw crap around. When monkeys feel threatened, scared, or anxious, they may throw their crap at you—or at each other. Human or primate, slinging crap around always ends the same way: in a mess.

# Promote Good Karma

**E**ver notice that the more good stuff you send out to the world, the more good stuff you share in? If so, you know something about how karma works. The word *karma* translates into "action" in the ancient language of Sanskrit, and it's a concept that has Buddhist and Hindu roots. The idea behind it is that good actions lead to good luck and bad actions lead to bad luck, throughout your life (and future lives, if you believe in reincarnation).

So, according to the law of karma, if you dish out crap to someone, you can expect to get crapped on in the near or distant future. If, however, you are cool to the people around you, you will have an easier time yourself. If you choose to be a person who is big- rather than small-hearted, kind rather than cruel, and forgiving rather than spiteful, you are promoting good karma. And that's a great way to break the crap cycle.

# Don't Blame Your Crap on Others

**S**o, you didn't get the lead in the school play. And then you spent the next semester accusing the girl who did get it of blatantly kissing the director's butt, instead of just accepting the situation and polishing your chops for the next tryout. Or maybe you're still blaming your parents for the fact that you're single (they bought you a crappy bike, not a car, for your 16th birthday) instead of perfecting your own personal brand of charm.

It may seem easier to point the finger at external stuff and people for all of life's crappy disappointments, but it's also a great way to keep the crap cycle going. Because if you think that all of the crap in your life is someone else's fault, then you will continue to give crap to them, even if only on a subconscious level. Then they will give it back to you, and on and on and on.

Instead, own the blame for things that are your fault. Or, better yet, don't blame anyone at all. Just accept the situation for what it is and move forward.

> **66** There's man all over
> for you, blaming on
> his boots the fault
> of his feet.
>
> —Samuel Beckett,
> Irish playwright and novelist
> (1906–1989)

## Tweet, Tweet, Plop

Baby birds don't wear diapers, so their moms and pops have to carry their crap out the hard way—by mouth. So, the next time your parents are telling you how much crap you always give them, you can politely add that at least they don't have to dispose of it the way the parents of birds do. And, from time to time, thank them for all of the times they have cleaned up your crap. Gratitude is a great way to break the crap cycle.

## Paying for Crap

While most people hate receiving crap, some actually like it. In 2008, a pile of 130-million-year-old dinosaur dung sold at a New York auction for nearly $1,000.

# Spread Love Not Crap

**J**ust like being cut off in traffic can ruin someone's day, being tossed a handful of random niceness can really *make* someone's day. To help break the crap cycle, increase the universal happiness quotient by committing random acts of kindness as often as possible.

Here are a few suggestions to get you started.

- Smile at the first five people you see in the morning.

- Give your friends and family little thoughtful presents when you come across something you think they'll like, not just on birthdays and official Hallmark holidays.

# Breaking the Stank Cycle

* The next time you see someone with food in their teeth or a fly down, quietly reveal the problem so that he or she can take care of business. (This also means resisting the temptation to take a picture of the offense and post it online.)

* Buy some flowers or chocolates to give to someone you know who needs them.

* Pay the bridge toll for the person behind you.

After you start your kindness campaign, see if you notice any difference in the way the world seems to be treating you.

# Don't Avenge Your Crap

When someone gives you crap, the notion of payback can be very enticing. You may be tempted to key Mr. Math teacher's car after he called you out publicly for being a slacker, or you may find yourself scheming to date and then dump the little sister of the creep that hijacked your girl. But revenge comes with its downsides. It radically multiplies the probability that even more crap will be coming your way (read about karma on page 84). Plus, it's just not pretty for any of the parties involved.

You can't always stop people from dumping on you, and you can't always escape all the general dung out there. But you do have the power to choose how you act and react. So instead of wasting energy thinking about how to avenge those who have wronged you, use that energy to get on with it. Watching you live a life you love is punishment enough for all the miserable people out there who hate their lives and want some miserable company.

# Life After Crap
# (Not Really)

**S**o now you know a little more about crap. You've poked and prodded, dissected and analyzed it. Braved, quit, and buried it. Perhaps you've even managed to make the best of the worst of it.

But that, of course, doesn't mean it won't keep coming your way. Crap is a natural part of life. Its flow is constant. As soon as you get rid of one type of crap, another type surfaces. The good news is that, as you get older, you get better and better at dealing with it.

And remember that what seems like crap now may not be crap in the long run. So try your best to love your crap, especially when you can't leave it. Even the worst crap can be a teacher, an inspiration, a motivator, and a stepping stone to better things.

> 66 *What does not destroy me makes me stronger.* 99
>
> Friedrich Wilhelm Nietzsche,
> German philosopher
> (1844–1900)

# About the Authors

 **Erin Elisabeth Conley** is a freelance writer and editor who splits her time between Buenos Aires, Argentina, and Los Angeles, California. She is also the author of Zest Books' *Crush: A Girl's Guide to Being Crazy in Love*, *Dumped: A Girl's Guide to Happiness After Heartbreak*, and *Uncool: A Girl's Guide to Misfitting In*.

 **Karen Macklin** is a San Francisco-based writer and editor. She has written for more than a dozen publications, including *The New York Times*, *San Francisco Weekly*, and *Yoga Journal*. Karen also coauthored *Indie Girl: From Starting a Band to Launching a Fashion Company, Nine Ways to Turn Your Creative Talent Into Reality*.

 **Jake Miller** is a writer who lives in Boston, Massachusetts. He has contributed essay, articles, and reviews to a variety of publications including *The New York Times*. Jake also wrote *Decoding Mom: Making Sense of Her Moods, Her Methods, and Her Madness*.